What's inside...

page 4

page 20

page 18

Editor: Karen Brown. Designers: Darren Miles. Model Maker: Susie Johns. Artist: Mary Hall.

ART ATTACK

GRANDPA CLOCK!

12
9
3
6

HERE'S HOW TO MAKE A MINIATURE GRANDPA CLOCK.

1 Make the base by sealing stones in a square-shaped box and sticking a smaller box to the top.

2 Glue a long box on top of the base boxes and then glue another square-shaped box on top of this.

3 From thick cardboard, cut a circle for the clock face, a hat shape with a flat base and two ears. Stick these in place.

YOU WILL NEED:

Small boxes, long box, card, thin card, newspaper, sticky tape, PVA glue, paint, paper fastener.

4

Cover the structure with at least three layers of torn newspaper pasted on with diluted PVA glue, paying attention to all the joins and leave it to dry.

5

Cut a circle the same size as the clock face from thin card. Paint a funny face on it and draw on some numbers, make a hole in the centre and attach some clock hands made from card with a paper fastener. Now paint the clock, give it a shirt and tie. You may want to make it look like your own granddad! Finally, attach the clock face onto the clock.

SUPER SEAHORSE!

USE YOUR IMAGINATION TO BRING THIS SEAHORSE TO LIFE!

YOU WILL NEED:

Card, glue, scissors, paints, coloured pens, glitter glue, sequins.

1 Trace the seahorse on the opposite page and stick it onto thin card.

2 Decorate it as you wish. You can use paint, or felt tip pens. Add glitter and sequins for some underwater shimmer!

wax crayon

IF YOU WANT TO MAKE SEVERAL DIFFERENT PICTURES, PHOTOCOPY THE PAGE!

6

7

TERRIFIC TEXTURES!

Apply a thick layer of acrylic paint and, while it's wet, quickly draw an old biro or piece of stick through the paint, to make stripes. This is a good technique for creating clothes patterns or a path.

You can get a really good texture by mixing something into the paint before you apply it to paper. In this case, I used rolled oats. You can create a muddy field or a stony beach. Adding sand is another way of creating a terrific texture!

Instead of using a brush to apply the paint, use a plastic knife. Here, the serrated blade of the knife makes furrows in the paint - a good effect for creating a ploughed field or making a roof look textured.

HERE ARE SIX WAYS TO CREATE EXCITING PAINT TEXTURES
- PERHAPS YOU CAN THINK OF MORE OF YOUR OWN?
PRACTICE THE TECHNIQUES ON SCRAPS OF PAPER THEN
USE THEM IN YOUR PICTURES!

Apply a thick layer of paint on to paper
or card and then scrape patterns in it,
while still wet, using the prongs of
a plastic fork. Use this technique to
create waves in a sea painting or
a fence round a house.

Using a flat brush, dab the paint thickly
on to the paper, creating an effect which
artists call 'impasto.' This rough, stippled
texture looks like a roughly plastered wall.

Cover the paper in paint and let it dry.
Make a small cone of paper - greaseproof
paper works best - and drop some paint
inside. Now squeeze the paint out of the
point of the cone and create squiggles and
swirls as if you were icing a cake.

ROOM WITH A VIEW!

CREATE A CHEERFUL VIEW THROUGH A FAKE WINDOW AND ALWAYS WAKE UP TO GOOD WEATHER!

1 Cut a large piece of card from a big cardboard box to make the base. Paint a background picture on some paper and stick on the base.

2 Create a frame with the long, narrow boxes. Secure them together with sticky tape.

Stick more long, narrow boxes in the middle in a cross shape to form the centre frame. If you don't have enough boxes, you can use strips of card.

4 Cover this frame with two layers of papier mâché and leave it to dry. Paint it with a couple of layers of white paint to cover the newspaper.

5 Stick the frame to the base with plenty of PVA glue and leave to dry.

6 Take two pieces of scrap fabric and cut them into rectangles. Fold them into loose concertinas and glue one short edge to the top of the frame. Do this to both sides. Use a bit of fabric as a tie back for each curtain. Finally hang on the wall!

SPLAT ATTACK!

1 Make some paper pulp. Mix up some diluted PVA glue - about 1 part PVA to 2 parts water - in a bowl. Add small pieces of torn newspaper and leave to soak for 20 minutes.

2 Spread out a plastic carrier bag. Take a handful of paper pulp and drop it on the carrier bag.

3 With your fingertips, mould the pulp splat into shape, smoothing the surface as you go.

4 Put the splats in a warm ventilated place and leave to dry for a few days.

5 When they're dry, you can smooth the rough edges with a bit of sandpaper. Then paint them! Give them funny faces and stick on googly eyes.

MAKE AS MANY DIFFERENT SIZED SPLATS AS YOU LIKE!

13

THINGS TO DO WITH

Why don't you get everyone you know to save old stamps? You can recycle them into some fun Art Attacks or better still, collect them for charity!

STAMP SNAKE

RECYCLE OLD STAMPS INTO A SSSILLY SSSNAKE.

You'll have to save a lot of stamps for this one! Soak them off the envelopes and let them dry. Then carefully thread them on to a piece of cotton with a large needle, making sure that the end of the cotton is knotted.

When you have threaded on enough stamps to make a snake, thread on a large bead and knot the other end of cotton. Finally paint some eyes on to the bead.

IN THE FRAME

HERE'S A UNIQUE WAY TO PERSONALISE AN ART ATTACK FRAME.

Take an old flat frame or make one from card and transform it by covering it with old stamps.

Use PVA glue to stick stamps all over the frame - mix up coloured stamps with paler ones.

Finally cover the whole thing with a thin layer of PVA glue to give it a nice finish.

OLD STAMPS!

STAMP SKETCHES

YOU DON'T EVEN HAVE TO TAKE THE STAMPS OFF THE ENVELOPES.

Bring stamps to life with a funny cartoon drawing. Look at the stamp and add a suitable body, hat or anything else.

Stick to old stamps - don't send them through the post after you have drawn around them.

STAMP BOX

PUT YOUR OWN STAMP ON A MEMENTO BOX.

Cover gift boxes or little trinket boxes with lots of stamps - the same way as you made the frame. Brush a thin layer of PVA glue over it to seal them down. Remember to leave the lid up or off while it dries.

PICTURE POSTAGE

CREATE SOME GIANT STAMPS FOR THE BEDROOM WALL

Here's a simple but fun idea. Make huge stamp pictures! Just copy a stamp onto a piece of paper and colour it in. When you have finished, stick it on to thin card then carefully go around the edge with scissors making the edges curvy like real stamps.

wing it!

MAKE THIS DRAGONFLY DAZZLE WITH COLOUR! DECORATE IT ANY WAY YOU WISH. YOU COULD USE FELT TIPS, GLITTER PAINTS, SEQUINS, COLLAGE, FABRIC, ANYTHING!

GET TRACING...

Start by tracing off the dragonfly shape and transferring it onto plain paper or card. If you plan to decorate it in different ways then trace it several times. (You can always photocopy it.)

MAKE IT SPARKLE...

Now decorate it any way you wish. What about colouring in the body with felt tips then using different coloured glitter all over the wings? You will need to brush on some PVA glue then sprinkle on glitter. Let it dry and shake off the excess. Keep doing this until the wings are covered. When it is completely dry use a black marker pen to add details and outline the sections on the wings. Finally, glue some sequins on for some extra sparkle!

OTHER IDEAS...

Alternatively, what about sticking on pieces of colourful scrap paper? Tear small pieces out from old magazines and stick on with paper glue. You can even use old bits of fabric cut into small pieces, coloured tissue, sweet wrappers or kitchen foil.

17

M∞-ney Box!

HERE'S A MOO-VALOUS WAY TO STORE YOUR POCKET MONEY!

1 Blow up a balloon to the size you want your cow's body to be. Stand it in a bowl to steady it and cover it with five layers of papier mâché. Leave it to dry until it's rock hard.

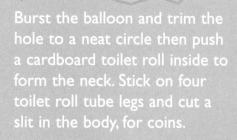

Burst the balloon and trim the hole to a neat circle then push a cardboard toilet roll inside to form the neck. Stick on four toilet roll tube legs and cut a slit in the body, for coins.

2

3 For the head, cut off the bottom corners from a small, shallow box and glue on a round cheese box lid. Add ears cut from cardboard and glue the head to the neck.

4 Cover the model with three layers of papier mâché and leave it to dry. Then paint it white all over.

18

YOU WILL NEED:

5

Paint the cow any colour you like. Snip a strip of tissue paper into a fringe and glue it to the head. Poke in a pipe cleaner tail, and add a tissue paper tassel to the end.

19

FAKE CAKE!

CAN'T BAKE? JUST FAKE! MAKE THIS ART ATTACK BIRTHDAY CAKE FOR SOMEONE SPECIAL!

1

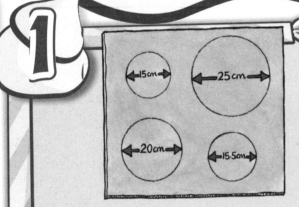

Cut four circles out of thick card, one 25cm in diameter, one 20cm, one 15.5cm and one 15cm. You could use compasses to draw the circles, or different sized plates.

2

Cut three strips of bendy card, 7cm wide to form the sides of the cake. (Leave them long and trim to fit later.) Cut a strip 3cm wide for the lid.

3

Cut a 30cm square base. Make the bottom cake tier by attaching a strip of card to the largest circle by taping it to the edges. Stick this to the base.

4

Tape another cardboard strip to the medium-sized circle and fix this to the top of the bottom cake tier with sticky tape. Tape another strip to the 15cm circle and stick this to the top, circle-side down.

YOU WILL NEED:

different sized plates
or pair of compasses,
thick cardboard,
drinking straws,
newspaper, sticky tape,
bendy card, kitchen roll,
PVA glue, pencil,
ruler, paint, string,
ribbon.

5 Tape the 3cm strip to the 15.5cm circle to make the lid. Make sure the lid fits loosely on top of the cake.

6 Cover the whole cake with three layers of torn newspaper pasted on with diluted PVA glue, paying attention to all the joins and keeping it neat. Leave it to dry.

Add a little more water to the diluted PVA and add some torn kitchen paper. Leave it to soak until you have a gooey pulp. Take small peanut-sized lumps, mould them with your fingertips and stick them around the edges of each cake tier to form icing.

8 To make candles, cut drinking straws into equal pieces and push a length of string through the centre of each one. Wrap each straw with a strip of torn paper brushed with diluted PVA glue. Stick the candles to the lid using the pulp.

9 Paint the cake white all over and let it dry. (You may need a couple of coats.) Paint the icing and candles. Write a message on top of the cake with paint. Leave it to dry.

FINALLY TIE SOME RIBBON ROUND EACH CAKE TIER. YOU CAN FILL THE TOP CAKE WITH SWEETS BEFORE GIVING TO SOMEONE AS A BIRTHDAY TREAT!

MAKE A MARK!

KEEP YOUR PAGE WITH ONE OF THESE QUICK AND EASY TO MAKE BOOKMARKS!

Draw cartoon people on card and cut them out. Colour them in and then cut slits under the arms so they slip on to the top of the page.

Attach colourful card fish to the end of pieces of string or strong thread. Add a bead or plastic ring to the other end.

Cut out two heart-shaped pieces of card. Stick lots of pieces of ribbon to one heart and then stick the other heart on top. Attach beads and hearts to the other ends of the ribbon.

HOME SWEET HOME!

side
↕ 9cm
↔ 14cm

side

back **front**
19cm ↕
9cm ↕
↔ 22cm

roof

roof
↕ 14cm
↔ 17cm

21cm ↕
↔ 30cm

1 Cut all the pieces you need from thick cardboard. Measure the pieces accurately using a ruler so they all fit together.

2 Stick the pieces together and stick the house to the base. Cut out a front door (11cm x 5cm) and two windows (4cm square) and stick them to the front.

3 Stick a short length of tube in place for a chimney and thin strips of card to make window and door frames. Add a small piece for a doorstep.

4 Stick circles of card or bottle tops to the roof and drinking straws to prop up the roof corners and along the roof join.

CREATE A TASTY-LOOKING GINGERBREAD HOUSE!

YOU WILL NEED:

Cardboard, sticky tape, PVA glue, newspaper, straws, bottle tops, cardboard tube, paints.

5 Cover the whole thing with three layers of papier maché and leave to dry. Now paint it brightly. Make it look like it's covered with sweets!

PVA

ART ATTACK

SNACK ATTACK!

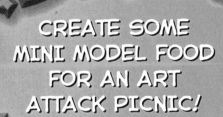

CREATE SOME
MINI MODEL FOOD
FOR AN ART
ATTACK PICNIC!

ASK AN ADULT TO HELP!

Salt dough recipe!

PLAIN FLOUR, SALT, WATER,
VEGETABLE OIL.

1. Mix together equal amounts of the flour and salt.
2. Add a little oil and enough water to make a dough.
3. Use your hands to knead the mixture into a soft dough ball.
4. Use the dough straight away to make models or store it, wrapped in cling film, in the fridge, for up to three days.
5. Leave your models to harden for a couple of days before painting them.

CLEANING DIRECTIONS

If you get the dough in carpet or on your clothes: allow the dough to dry, then remove it with a loose brush and/or vacuum. If necessary, rinse with gentle soap, cold water and a brush.

START!

1 Break off pieces of dough, roll it into balls to create oranges and tomatoes. Roll it into long sausage shapes to make a cucumber or bananas. Squash both ends flat to make a drinks can.

2 Roll a larger piece into a ball and then flatten it on either side to make a cake. Carefully cut a slice out of the cake to make it look real. Flatten a ball of dough to make a pizza.

3 You can copy the other things in the picture or create some of your own favourite food.

4 When you have moulded your shapes, simply leave them to dry overnight before painting.

5 Finally use a scrap piece of fabric or a hanky to make a picnic rug.